What Makes Us Episcopalians?

John E. Booty

Morehouse-Barlow Co., Inc.
Wilton, Connecticut

*Morehouse-Barlow Co., Inc.
78 Danbury Road
Wilton, Connecticut 06897*

ISBN 0-8192-1302-0

Printed in the United States of America

Contents

Preface

This small book reprints for wider use a series of articles commissioned by and printed in *The Episcopalian.* The subject matter was dictated in a large part by the conviction that over against distorting voices and tendencies there was need to explore our identity as Episcopalians and as members of world-wide Anglicanism. Our identity consists of many things, not the least being the comprehensive nature of our tradition and the way in which people of great diversity are united by a common recognition of Scripture, Tradition, Reason and Experience as authoritative in all that we think, say and do. The comprehensiveness of the Episcopal Church is not placid and sterile, as some believe. It is characterized by a creative tension constituted by the dynamic interaction of the four poles of authority. This creative tension at times strains and threatens to break the bonds of charity as divers people emphasize one or another of the poles to the exclusion of the others. The threat of schism recurs time and again in the midst of discussions, controversies and confusion, the inevitable consequences of a living church pursuing its mission in a constantly changing society. As Episcopalians we strive to hold to and justly honor the authority of Scripture, Tradition, Reason and Experience in the right proportion, giving full weight to each, acknowledging the proper authority due to each one in their relation one to another. We acknowledge, as we do this, the tension between them and recognize in that tension a creative dynamism. The tension is at times disturbing and sometimes verges upon the intolerable, but it provides to us a lively dynamism and makes it possible for us to adapt to the new without denying the values of the old. That we don't always succeed, that the interactions and tensions are complex and beyond the ken of many, and that being an Episcopalian can be hard work is admitted and I hope illuminated in the following pages. It is this very creative tension that appeals to many questing people in our complex and dangerous era as not only viable but necessary.

Continuous education, through the entire stretch of life, is obviously of vital importance to Episcopalians as they make day-to-day decisions in relation to Scripture, Tradition, Reason and Experience. It is hoped that this little book may serve as a tool in such education. There has already been some use made of the articles as a basis for study and discussion. There are six chapters, the first is introductory and presents some historical background, introducing the main themes, the next four are given over to separate considerations of Scripture, Tradition, Reason and Experience, and the last is a conclusion and reflects on where we have been in the course of our study and on the meaning or meanings of it all. The book could be the basis for a six week study course, during Lent or at some other convenient time. The study leader might want to draw up questions for discussion and assign different members of the study group to begin discussion when the group meets by means of a brief consideration of the question or questions. The study leader might take that responsibility, summarizing the chapter very briefly and initiating discussion. The book could be used in various other ways, in connection with an inquirers class, or it could be put in the hands of individuals who express concern for the matter with which it is concerned. My additional hope is that this small study of great subjects may inspire further adult education projects. In particular, as I remark in the conclusion, I am concerned to see basic Christian education in the Episcopal Church "structured and conducted in terms of the creative interplay of the four vital elements"—Scripture, Tradition, Reason and Experience.

I am indebted to Janette Pierce of *The Episcopalian* who came to me with the idea for this book and to Judy Mathe Foley, of the same publication, who patiently and expertly edited my typescript. I am grateful to the Rev. Theodore A. McConnell for suggesting that the articles be reprinted in this form and to Anne Doherty for her editorial assistance. Lastly, I am thankful for having been born in and sustained by the Episcopal Church with its appreciation of Scripture, Tradition, Reason and Experience and of the creative tension which their interaction inspires.

John E. Booty

Chapter 1. Roots in England; Testing in America

We use four strands
of authority to search
for truth: Scripture, Tradition,
Reason, Experience.

How do Episcopalians in the twentieth century know what is true? How do we choose a course of action? How do we make wise decisions? Who are we? How did we become this way?

To answer these questions, Episcopalians look to Holy Scripture. We interpret what we read there in the tradition not only of the Church of the first five or six centuries, but also of the Church of England in the sixteenth and seventeenth centuries. Then we try to understand, using reason—that rational, critical capability which is a significant part of what it means to be created in the image of God—and experience—that which we learn through living, working, loving and dying in the present.

Scripture, tradition, reason and experience all contribute to our quest as members of the Church to know the truth and do it.

Interwoven and interdependent, these four strands or elements of authority sometimes seem to fly apart as, given the human condition and the power of God's grace, individuals and groups emphasize one or discount another.

In the Church great effort is expended to maintain all groups with their differing views in dialogue with each other. When this fails, the bond of love dies, and we are in schism. But when disparate individuals and groups stay together, speak earnestly with one another of things that matter to them, and listen with great care to what others are saying, then out of this creative tension comes a harmony, a music that carries us to the truth and to action that most nearly corresponds to the truth.

This particular dynamic relationship of Scripture, tradition, reason and experience that characterizes the Episcopal Church began in sixteenth century England at the time of the Reformation. During the reigns of Henry VIII, Edward VI and Elizabeth I, the English Reformation began, developed, and matured so that by the beginning of the seventeenth century people had become accustomed to the change, internalized the results, and acknowledged a tradition subsequently called Anglican.

Thomas Cranmer, Archbishop of Canterbury under Kings Henry and Edward, with the first official English Bible in print, provided *The Book of Common Prayer* and the Articles of Religion. Both emphasized the overwhelming importance of Scripture as containing all that is necessary to salvation. Like Luther and Calvin, Cranmer sought to remove all that obscured the Word of God in Scripture and in those visible words, the sacraments of baptism and Holy Communion.

Grounded in the reform movement, Anglicans needed a way to distinguish between things essential and non-essential to salvation. This they sought to do through the use of reason or what English humanists called "right reason" because it was not mere rationalism, but rather Spirit-filled reason. Richard Hooker called it "the moral law of reason."

Cranmer attacked superstitious abuses not only because they had no basis in Scripture, but also because they were irrational and immoral. He, along with such Christian humanists as Desiderius Erasmus of Rotterdam, desired only that people might live by the precepts of the Gospel to build a Christian society.

English reformers retained from the Church of their youth that which could be proven ancient by reference to early church writings, and they therefore opposed the Puritans who condemned everything associated with the Middle Ages and thus with the Church of Rome. Consequently, as they sought to suppress all that inhibited the working of God's Word, they did away with minor orders and denied the authority of the Bishop of Rome. The English Church retained the threefold ministry of bishop, priest and deacon, and the Prayer Book consecration in Holy Communion retained much of the Canon of the Mass in a way no other non-Roman Church did.

Queen Elizabeth I let her Puritan subjects know she did not agree with them, and Richard Hooker, sixteenth century theologian, supported her with reasonable arguments for toleration. The Anglican roots of reformation and Christian humanism were nourished by the earliest Christian tradition as transmitted through the medieval Church but cleansed of superstition and corruption.

These roots were nourished, too, by the experience of the reformers and of those for whom they labored. The sixteenth century was an age of great personal peril, a time of plagues and warfare, for which the dance of death was a chilling symbol. It was also an age of great social distress, inflation out of control, agriculture and husbandry undergoing costly changes, and the poor increasing in number, in suffering, and in restlessness.

The Scripture was read; the Word was preached; sacraments were administered; discipline was meted out in large part to condemn injustice, to minister to suffering, and to lead the people of God into the construction of a godly kingdom. The Prayer Book emphasized Communion—with God and with neighbors—requiring communicants to cleanse themselves of their sins by the grace of God in Christ who died that they might be made new. The Prayer Book rhythm of repentance and thanksgiving was meant to affect personal and social behavior. Anglicanism was rooted in the realities of the time and in the experience gained by both the leaders and those whose fate it was to be led.

In an important sense, the history of Anglicanism from the sixteenth century to the present is a history of the four strands or elements, the bases of authority, and of the individuals and groups that represent them.

In the Church of England in the seventeenth century, the Puritans and Calvinists championed scriptural authority, and the Laudians sought to instill a greater respect for tradition; the Cambridge Platonists emphasized the importance of right reason, the "candle of the Lord"; and one might suggest that in striving to maintain the most intimate relationship between religion and the new science, the botanist John Ray and the chemist/physicist Robert Boyle testified to the importance of experience for the Church of England and its members. But all acknowledged the necessity of all four elements.

In the eighteenth century, the Evangelical Revival, which Wesley and Whitfield led, sought to free Scripture from bondage to tradition, rationalism, and the corrosive errors of deists and atheists. They sought to emphasize its centrality in relation to tradition, right reason and experience, maintaining what William Meade, third Bishop of Virginia, called the "law of proportion"—loving the Church, its ministry, and its sacraments without elevating any of them to the level of Scripture.

In the nineteenth century, tradition was emphasized anew by Tractarians and by the Anglo-Catholics who followed them. But John Henry Newman from the pulpit of St. Mary's, Oxford, explored the necessary use of reason, and John Henry Hobart, Bishop of New York, proclaimed, "Evangelical the High Churchman must be!"

So-called liberals such as Frederick Temple and Mark Pattison, contributors to the controversial *Essays and Reviews* (1860), insisted on the critical use of reason and tradition to interpret Scripture. To some they appeared to be attacking Scripture in such a way as to deny divine inspiration although Benjamin Jowett in his essay, "On the Interpretation of Scripture," was trying, like Erasmus before him, to free the scriptures from the obscurities in which scholastic theologians had buried them, that the faithful might be awakened to "the mind of Christ in Scripture."

None of these groups could escape taking experience into account. The Evangelicals and Tractarians at times seemed to concentrate solely on *personal* religious experience; but the Evangelicals fought for the abolition of the slave trade and against slavery itself, and the Tractarians, chiefly through their successors, the Anglo-Catholics, sought to minister to the poor in urban slums. The Christian Socialists in England and the Social Gospelers in America so emphasized experience in their struggle to convert society from ruthless competition for profit to practical cooperation for mutual welfare that they stand forth as champions of experience.

Frederick D. Maurice (1805-1872) in England and Vida Scudder (1861-1954) in America are representative of those who sought to confront the challenges of modern society while adhering to the heritage contained in Scripture and tradition. Maurice's aim was to socialize Christianity and to Christianize socialism. Scudder, Wellesley professor from one of the first families of New England, highly educated, steeped in English literature, an ardent feminist and socialist as well as theologian, was outraged by injustice.

The American scene provides experiences peculiar to our place on planet earth, and here, perhaps, the harmony of this quartet of elements of authority is most severely tested. The nineteenth and twentieth centuries have seen the Episcopal Church both enriched and troubled by them. The separation of Church and state together with proliferation of Churches and sects—all in tension but all compelled to live together—the amazing mixture of races and ethnic groups, the conquest of the frontier through the eighteenth and nineteenth centuries and the conquest of space in the twentieth, rapid economic and industrial growth and the force of the idea of progress, the challenges of world power and global crisis, the struggle for civil rights and women's liberation, and much, much more have influenced the environment in which Scripture is read, tradition is received, and reason operates. All in one way or another differentiate the Episcopal Church from the Church of England. And one can safely say that where Anglicanism is creative and lively, tensions will exist.

The interplay of elements persists, and American Episcopalians struggle to live creatively through and in present experience while maintaining fidelity to Scripture as the rule of their lives, tradition as the interpretation of that rule, and reason as the God-given but far from perfect instrument by which we apprehend the truth and do it.

In this book, I explore each of these four strands of authority without artificially isolating one from the others, rather focusing on one in the midst of the others, trying to discover just what makes us Episcopalians.

Without ignoring our English heritage, I shall concentrate on the American experience. Dialogue with our history should help us to understand our past and recognize influences that have shaped us and help us to decide on the basis of Scripture, as interpreted by tradition, in the light of our experience, by the operation of God-given reason what is essential and what is non-essential, what should be adhered to at all costs, and what should change with changing times, people, and other circumstances.

The Gospel frees us from the tyranny of lesser things, frees us to serve God and our neighbors and thus to obtain that measure of human dignity and creativity which were ours at creation. Christianity is a faith deeply involved with history. Anglicanism from the beginning has acknowledged the importance of history. This appreciation is not a dedication to antiquarianism, but a result of our encounter with God in history, through Word and sacrament, ever working in history to judge and save us.

Chapter 2. Scripture Unfolds God's Sacred Drama

We are a Bible Church through and through.

In 1801, after much discussion and some amendment, the General Convention of the Episcopal Church adopted the Thirty-Nine Articles of Religion, first authorized by Convocation of the Church of England in 1563. In so doing, the Episcopal Church affirmed the authority of Scripture in an article which reads: "Holy Scripture containeth all things necessary to salvation: so that whatsoever is not read therein, nor may be proved thereby, is not to be required of any man, that it should be believed as an article of Faith, or be thought requisite or necessary to salvation."

This affirmation echoes the conviction of sixteenth century reformers such as Thomas Cranmer that Scripture, not "unwritten traditions," possesses supreme authority for faith. In affirming this principle, the fledgling Episcopal Church reached back through the sixteenth century, beyond the Middle Ages to the early Church which cherished Scripture and maintained its authority against claims of false prophets and erroneous doctrine.

While all in the Church of England were required to subscribe to this article on Scripture, not all understood it in the same way. Some Puritans claimed no one should so much as pick a straw from the ground without express warrant of Scripture. Richard Hooker, sixteenth century theologian, opposed such Puritans, saying Scripture presupposes the operation of reason, God-given "right reason," and was given in order to set aright what God had created good but Adam had crippled by sin.

Furthermore, Scripture is received and transmitted, studied and interpreted in the Church in history. Scripture is the Church's greatest treasure. The Church, subservient to Scripture, is the guardian of that treasure.

Francis White, writing in 1635, said the primitive Church is a "conduit pipe to derive and convey to succeeding generations the celestial water contained in Holy Scripture." Michael Ramsey, 100th Archbishop of Canterbury, said the sixteenth century Church of England avoided the error of the Calvinists, who sought to place Scripture in a "self-contained logical system," and saw that it "centers simply in the fact of Christ himself, and this fact is to be apprehended with the aid of the whole structure and tradition of the Church."

In the newly-formed Episcopal Church the Evangelicals were chiefly responsible for the affirmation of Scripture's supremacy. They believed Scripture is sufficient because it is the inspired Word of God, containing all that is necessary to salvation and because, when regarded in its entirety, it is the complete revelation of God's truth, needing no supplement.

Charles McIlvaine (1799-1873), the evangelical Bishop of Ohio, asserted that any denial that Scripture is God's self-revelation undercuts Christian faith and should be denounced. He said this while aware of the rise of historical biblical criticism, of Darwin's theory of evolution by means of natural selection, and of John Stuart Mill's provision of a natural basis for moral conduct—all widely regarded as threatening Scripture's supremacy.

Some Evangelicals reacted to these threats by clinging persistently to the belief that Scripture was verbally inspired—every word—and without error. Some left the Episcopal Church. Others accepted the contributions of biblical criticism and made peace with natural science. In so doing, the last conformed to a long-standing tradition.

With remarkable consistency Anglicanism echoes Richard Hooker's insistence that Scripture presupposes God's acting in nature and through human reason. Scripture is essential in relation to our ultimate salvation for without God's revelation in Jesus the Christ as witnessed to and conveyed by Scripture, nature is marred, reason corrupted and humanity is doomed.

But, said John Wilkins, a seventeenth century Bishop of Chester, the Bible is not concerned with scientific data. If it refers to the sun's rising, it is not thereby making a statement concerning astronomy: It is simply reflecting the common understanding at the time of writing.

In trying to maintain the authority properly due Scripture while at the same time fixing the limits of that authority, people took different positions, sometimes so opposed as to endanger the peace of the Church. The opposing parties were both to some degree right and to some degree wrong. The truth seemed to be most completely expressed in the crossfire, at the point of greatest tension.

How does the Episcopal Church now view Scripture? The Thirty-Nine Articles of Religion still exist, and most of us would assent to what they claim for Scripture, but in our assent we would no doubt express ourselves differently.

For some the Scriptures are daily sustenance—read, studied, prayed over, and used in decision-making. This does not mean such people take everything they say to be literally true, nor does it mean they set Scripture over against science when science is operating within its proper domain.

On the other hand, some agree that Scripture contains all things necessary to salvation but find the language, thought patterns, and much else foreign and largely irrelevant. Those people may seek their sustenance in liturgy, private devotions, corporate experience, or in some other way in which Scripture may be involved importantly but not revered, and they may be without any keen sense of Scripture as the Word of God active in the world. Such variety of opinion necessitates constant conversation about Scripture's inspiration and authority.

When I take the Bible in hand, I know it is a library of books of great diversity, books written by numerous and diverse people using different sources. I know, too, the authors were affected by their times and circumstances and that not everything they wrote is of equal value or is inspired as our ancestors believed. The Bible is a human product.

The Old Testament was the Bible of the earliest Christians, but its exact contents varied. The New Testament is composed of those writings that preserved the early Church's memory of what God had done through Jesus. The first collection of writings contained the works that survived the test of fidelity to the revelation of God in Christ Jesus. Many other works were proposed and rejected and are now called apochryphal.

We must understand that the Church, acting in accordance with the Holy Spirit, produced Scripture and decreed its authority on the basis of its experience. That is to say, the early Christians, through reading and hearing scriptural works, with all their cultural conditioning and sometimes difficult and imprecise language, retained a lively memory of God's acting in Christ and, together with their liturgy in which Scripture was prominent, knew he was not dead and gone, but risen and active in their midst, reconciling them to God and to one another. We say this is the work of the Holy Spirit because where such memory and lively power exist, there the Spirit is active.

To use different words, Scripture is authoritative because as literature, with all the limitations of human frailty and finitude, the works that compose the Bible convey to us the history of God's activity, witnessing to God's creating, seeking out, calling, covenanting with, judging, loving, saving the people who are his own.

Central to the Bible is a powerful drama we represent in songs, creeds, liturgies and various other ways. Eucharistic Prayer B in *The Book of Common Prayer* provides a striking example: "We give thanks to you, O God, for the goodness and love which you have made known to us in creation; in the calling of Israel to be your people; in your Word spoken through the prophets; and above all in the Word made flesh . . . ."

This is the great drama which, remembered, draws us into its orbit and affects our lives not only in ultimate, but in everyday, concrete ways. We are expected, then, and Scripture presupposes that we shall, to use our reason and all other useful tools available to study Scripture, to examine and lay bare the essential, sacred drama, and to participate in it as it penetrates our minds and hearts.

Is Scripture the Word of God? It is insofar as in the sacred drama God speaks and enables those to whom he speaks to respond. As God's "Word," enabling human response, John the Evangelist named Jesus "The Word of God." Scripture is the "Word of God" insofar as God speaks to us through its human words, enabling our response. This, then, is the creative Word, for God's Word in and through Scripture reaches out to effect saving change in us.

People have difficulty in understanding this definition because it is not empirically provable, but as the Doctrine Commission of the Church of England says, no one who earnestly strives to be Christian can avoid struggling with Scripture as a part of the tradition with which we must come to terms. And when we do so, whatever our presuppositions, we "find there 'words of eternal life'."

Viewed in terms of the dynamic, lively Word of God not only to peoples past, but to those present, speaking through a drama that persists, drawing us into its very heart, engaging us in a history which is still unfolding, influenced not only by the past, but by the beckoning future, the Bible is not static and lifeless or rigid and stifling. Since it involves personal communication, the Spirit causing creative encounter, it will not communicate to each of us in the same fashion with identical messages. We should expect variations of understanding from widely differing Christians.

What Scripture "means" to a twentieth century middle-class American may differ from what it means to a Ugandan living in the power of the "biblical" drama enacted between Idi Amin and the martyred Archbishop Janani Luwum. When the American and the Ugandan share their understanding of God's Word in Scripture, they will both speak of the drama of God's acts in history culminating in Jesus the Christ through whose Spirit they meet.

As the Doctrine Commission says, "The New Testament itself handed on to the Church a volume of unfinished business. Within its pages we can see issues being shaped, ideas coming into being. The process could not, did not, stop when the writer of II Peter . . . laid down his pen.

"The Bible is often not relevant to our problems because the precise questions to which it addresses itself are not those which we would wish to put. But it did inaugurate a tradition within which those problems can be handled—and handled in a way which is in keeping with the spirit of the Bible.

"This surely is one major role of the Holy Spirit. Scripture has to be filled out by prayer and thought and the ongoing life and witness of the Church. The resources at our disposal are the Bible plus the use made of it in the Christian community down the ages."

Taking seriously the article of religion adopted in 1801 means we shall all be serious students of the Bible by the use of reason, tradition and experience, immersing ourselves in its central drama, open to God's speaking to us in the present unfolding of that drama, not searching for specific answers to specific questions, but so immersed in Scripture in company with the rest of the faithful in the Church that we are enabled to make decisions that reflect the mind of Christ.

The Episcopal Church is a Bible Church. Its liturgy is through and through biblical; its clergy consent to the Bible's authority as "the Word of God" containing "all things necessary to salvation" and promise to be faithful in reading and studying Holy Scripture; and on one Sunday each year all of us pray, "Blessed Lord, who caused all Holy Scriptures to be written for our learning; Grant us so to hear them, read, mark, learn and inwardly digest them, that we may embrace and ever hold fast the blessed hope of everlasting life, which you have given us in our Savior Jesus Christ; who lives and reigns with you and the Holy Spirit, one God, for ever and ever. Amen."

Chapter 3. Tradition Illuminates the Mind of the Church

We look to tradition
to guide us
in knowing the truth.

Of what value is tradition? William White, first Bishop of Pennsylvania and a founder of both our nation and the Episcopal Church, answered: "As testimony extraneous to Scripture is the standard for trying of the authenticity of any of its books, so, in ascertaining the sense of any passage of an acknowledged book, we are not to shut our eyes against the light which beams on us from the same source."

Tradition, especially that of the early Church, was valuable to White but perplexes many Episcopalians. We find White's statement strange and ask what he means. We wonder about the value of tradition, the past history and wisdom of Christians and people in general. Do we really want to preserve and be influenced by what has gone before us?

When pressed, we may find we are of two minds. As Americans we cherish traditions of liberty and justice but are inclined to oppose traditions that inhibit progress and stifle creativity. As Episcopalians we cherish traditions associated with critical turning points in our spiritual pilgrimage but oppose traditions that quell our spirits and threaten our security.

Anglicanism knows something of this ambivalence. Our roots are in the sixteenth century struggle to recover the primacy of God's Word in matters concerning salvation. In the process, traditions—unwritten verities deemed necessary to salvation—were denounced. With the adoption in 1801 of the Thirty-Nine Articles of Religion, the American Church allowed that traditions might be useful but must be either rooted in Scripture or not repugnant to God's Word, and, if not found in Scripture, they must never be imposed as necessary to salvation.

Scripture was the prime authority, our assurance against error and the tyranny of those who invent ultimate truths and impose them on pain of eternal damnation. The principle of scriptural primacy also protects us against the snares of ecclesiastical infallibility. A. V. G. Allen, professor at Episcopal Theological School in Cambridge, Mass., at the beginning of this century, stated: "Infallibility is no longer to be held as a mark of the Church. Everything must be tested by the appeal to Scripture." The rites and ceremonies which the Church commends as useful must not be "contrary to God's Word written." The principle of *adiaphora,* "things indifferent," arises here, committing us to the arduous task of distinguishing between things essential to salvation—such as belief in Christ as Savior—and things indifferent—such as kneeling or standing for prayer. As a result we do not treat the latter as of equal authority with the former.

Having said this, we have still not considered all that lies before us. Reformers who denounced traditions, superstitious or indifferent, still appealed to tradition, and we do so today. Richard Field, the seventeenth century dean of Gloucester, identified various kinds of traditions ranging from rites and ceremonies to Scripture itself, the transmission of Scripture and its meaning through the ages, and "the sum of Christian religion contained in the Apostles' Creed"—all is tradition.

Richard Hooker in his *Lawes* referred to that which antiquity judged fit, and by the "long continued practice of the whole Church," as authoritative tradition. Indeed, Anglicanism from its inception has appealed to history and specifically to the first five or six centuries of the Church's life for proof against error and for direction in its affairs. But in making this appeal we have ever insisted that antiquity be tested by God's Word before being endowed with authority, especially in matters concerned with salvation.

The Oxford Movement of the so-called Tractarians in nineteenth century England and America emphasized tradition anew. In opposition to Protestants who claimed the Bible alone is the heart of religion and that every individual must discover its meaning for him or herself, the theologians of the Oxford Movement emphasized tradition in relation to the corporate authority of the Church.

Ferdinand C. Ewer (1826-83), Anglo-Catholic rector of St. Ignatius' Church, New York City, said, "From the day of its Pentecostal quickening, the Catholic Church, thus illuminated . . . with all necessary truth, has assumed the office among fallen and blind men and calmly performed the functions of the Infallible Teacher of the world." Ewer claimed the Church was prior to the New Testament, endowing the Church with truth. The Church transmits and interprets Scripture. Tradition is thus the life of the Church, not any particular doctrine issuing from it as sentences from a mouth. Tradition exists beside Scripture and incorporates it.

Frank J. Hall, professor at Western Theological Seminary in Chicago, spoke for and influenced generations of Anglo-Catholics through his voluminous *Dogmatics*. For Hall, as for Ewer, tradition was the Church in its dogmatic office transmitting the faith in purity and integrity from generation to generation. Hall believed emphasis on tradition did not stifle the working of the Spirit. The tradition *is* the Spirit illuminating the Church's Mind. He suggested five lines of transmission: "Scripture, consent, creeds, ancient literature, permanent institutions and the liturgy combine to make the ancient faith recognizable and have the effect of nullifying spurious traditions and teachings."

In addition, for many, including John Keble, tradition is not only preservative, but potentially revolutionary. Keble, one of the original Oxford Tractarians, turned back to primitive tradition not only to protect the deposit of faith once given to the saints, but to find the basis for what John Henry Newman called "the second reformation," the restoration of ancient beliefs and practices inspired by the Spirit in the ancient Church. Such restoration involved overturning established authority and quite possibly disobeying established laws—all in the name of Christian tradition which had been ignored or discarded by a people who were apostate.

As may be supposed, the English Reformers and later people such as Professor Allen would have problems with the Anglo-Catholic emphasis on tradition in relation to the Church's authority. American Evangelicals were clearly alarmed. William Meade, third Bishop of Virginia, insisted on subordinating the Church to Scripture. "The Church introduces us to the Scriptures, bidding us to read and learn this blessed book; and when it attempts to teach—though it may use creeds and catechisms and liturgies for brevity, convenience and worship—[it] teaches chiefly in and by God's own words, the plainest and best after all." The problem was not that Anglo-Catholics disdained Scripture—they most highly valued it as being at the core of sacred tradition—but rather in the eyes of the Evangelicals they tended to value the Church too much. The disagreement concerned emphasis, such emphasis as might touch the core of faith.

In the present century the most significant discussions of tradition have taken place in ecumenical settings and involve a careful consideration of definitions since, admittedly, the subject is difficult. Basic to all such conversations are three quite different understandings of tradition: (1) that which is handed down *(traditum),* including Scripture, creeds, liturgies, and the like; (2) the act of handing down *(actus tradendi);* and (3) the record of the handing down of the tradition, which is sacred history, providing a basis for Anglicanism's appeal to antiquity.

We must realize that here we are dealing with what is the heart of the Christian faith for as Albert Outler of Southern Methodist University has said, God's prime act of *traditum* was the handing over of "Jesus Christ to share our existence and to effect our salvation" (Rom. 8:31-32). This act or tradition is renewed by God's Spirit in every generation. "The Holy Spirit—'sent by the father in my name' (John 14:25)—re-recreates the original act of tradition (*traditum)* by an act of 'traditioning' (*actus tradendi)* so the tradition of Jesus

Christ becomes a living force in later lives and in faith based on response to contemporary witness."

The Church, as the locus of the Spirit, is thus involved in handing on, the act of traditioning, but the focus is not on the Church itself. The focus is on the tradition, on that which is handed down, and thus is uniquely on Jesus Christ, our *traditum.*

In 1963 the World Council of Churches' Faith and Order Commission reported on *Tradition and Traditions,* making a distinction between Tradition and traditions. Tradition is reality as it is in Jesus Christ, handed down through history, and traditions are the more or less temporary expressions of Tradition. We refer to Scripture and the life of the Church to distinguish between the two.

Scripture is dead, worthless, unless made living by the Spirit. This happens in the day-to-day life of the Church. Thus far nothing new is added concerning the reality of Christ. The WCC group said what we discern to be new is the *handing on* of the reality of Christ from generation to generation: "This communication does not involve creating fresh truth, but the bringing of the Gospel to bear upon fresh situations in history, requiring fresh formulations."

Scripture comes to life in the Church not just in words, but in the actions of daily life, enabling us to distinguish between Tradition and traditions, not always with great clarity and certainty, but, if we are sincerely engaged in relationship to Christ, sufficiently to maintain the proper relation between Tradition and traditions.

In these discussions we begin to see how tradition has been undergoing reexamination in this century. In 1976 the Anglican-Roman Catholic International Commission, with Bishop Arthur Vogel of West Missouri representing the Episcopal Church, issued a statement *(Truth and Authority)* which passed by as no longer tenable both the Protestant insistence on Scripture alone and the Roman Catholic insistence on two sources of revelation (Scripture and tradition) with some truth revealed in Scripture and not in tradition, some in tradition and not in Scripture. The commentators wrote: "In propounding the faith, the Church does not put forward under divine guidance facts which are not to be found in Scripture, but determines how the Gospel should be interpreted and obeyed. The true account of the relation between Scripture and tradition does not lie either in a literal *Scriptura sola* [Scripture alone] theory or in a theory of 'Scripture *plus* tradition'; rather, a genuine tradition is always an interpretation of Scripture, and Scripture is accepted according to the interpretation of the Church's tradition."

In light of recent discussions, then, Scripture—God's Word—would seem to be at the core of tradition, elevated above all the rest that is regarded as tradition because in human experience the

Gospel is conveyed through reading and hearing Scripture. We find in the Bible "words of eternal life." But that Word must be handed on. Transmission involves not only the physical passing on of a book called the Holy Bible, but also interpreting God's Word in words and actions that convey the Gospel to the next generation.

This activity of communication is also tradition. The interpretations in words and actions—in writing, rites, ceremonies, individual and corporate ways of evangelizing and serving, and the like—are traditions subservient to Scripture and the fundamental activity of handing it on. Such traditions are more or less temporary because new circumstances demand new interpretations. Until replaced they are valued as vehicles of God's saving power in the world. Indeed, when communication or interpretation are most difficult, we rightly find ourselves relying on traditions from the past that retain power in the present.

Tradition in all these various senses is what we in the Episcopal Church mean when we say that next to Scripture tradition guides us in knowing what to believe and what to do as Christians. But for it to operate in the most beneficial way, we need to steep ourselves in the tradition in all its senses, learn it, hand it on, interpret it in the light of the present, and be constantly engaged in distinguishing between Tradition and traditions, never allowing the latter to detract from nor submerge the former. Traditions are of value only insofar as they serve to illuminate and transmit the Tradition that is Jesus Christ attested to in the pages of the Holy Bible.

Chapter 4. Faith Needs Reason and Reason Needs Grace

We are a people
who ask questions.

William White, first Bishop of Pennsylvania, was a learned and serious theologian who emphasized the role of reason in religion. This was natural given the importance of eighteenth century Enlightenment thought on his education and on the company of patriots who labored at Philadelphia to provide religious and philosophical foundations for the new nation.

The freshness of a rational and optimistic view of life and the universe pervaded the atmosphere in which White lived and worked. Humanity, with its inherent value and prospective achievement, was glorified in contrast to the Puritan, Calvinist emphasis on the depravity of the human race. The rationality of God's human creatures was celebrated with the correlative de-emphasis on scriptural revelation (especially concerning the miraculous) and churchly tradition (especially the moribund Old World traditions).

White, however, was not a wild-eyed rationalist as some believed Tom Paine to be; he was an Anglican who understood by reason what Richard Hooker and Jeremy Taylor understood. Reason does not exist in isolation; it is not omnicompetent, but rather exists in tension with Scripture and tradition and is subservient to God's Word.

Reason for White was a human faculty by which we judge what is presented to us through the senses. "God has adorned our nature," White wrote, "with an intellectual faculty, in reference to which it is said of Him—'who teaches us more than the beasts of the earth, and maketh us wiser than the fowls of the heaven.' "

And yet reason goes astray, misled by passion. Like the will, reason can and does rebel against being and doing that for which God created it—and humanity. Reason is in need of grace. This is especially evident when we acknowledge that reason does not naturally tend to knowledge of God and morality. Reason needs the revelation to which Scripture and tradition attest.

Sydney Temple summarized White's understanding: "Under the disposition of Grace the mind is freed from the control of the passions and is able to weigh the signs of God in all of nature, in history, and in direct revelation without error. Aid is given to the mind by the Holy Spirit as a 'holy agency,' applying what is thus received not irresistibly, but by an operation consistent with freedom— preventing [leading] us."

Since the sixteenth century Anglicanism has placed considerable emphasis on reason in relation to salvation. At first this emphasis was made because western tradition respected the function of reason in matters religious and because the concept of "right reason" was central to the teachings of the Christian humanism that so much influenced the rise and development of the Reformation and subsequent Anglicanism. Reason was emphasized equally because sixteenth century Anglicans came to acknowledge that in a certain kind—not all—of Puritanism, irrationalism was growing and threatening the religious settlement on which they took their stand.

Richard Hooker, the late sixteenth century theologian whose *Lawes of Ecclesiastical Polity* William White read while in college, was the most eloquent and forceful defender of the role of reason in Anglican authority during the Church's formative years. Against those who claimed God's will is made known solely and wholly through Scripture, Hooker argued that Scripture itself presupposes the operation of reason or, as he sometimes said, "the moral law of reason." Against those Puritans who claimed the direct inspiration of the Holy Spirit for what they did (and sometimes what they did could be justified neither by Scripture nor tradition), Hooker said either they must be prophets as of old or the Spirit must yield its reason. What is done—so Scripture presupposes—must be well reasoned and thus moral.

Hooker knew full well that sin cripples reason. We have no natural tendency toward truth and goodness which has not been so corrupted that it leads to falsehood and evil. Reason is in need of healing grace. That grace comes through Christ as revealed in Scripture. Under the influence of grace we test the spirits, using the rule of faith—Scripture and tradition, particularly the tradition of the early Church.

The insistence upon the operation of reason in Anglicanism is not without reason itself. Jeremy Taylor, in the seventeenth century, put the case well when he argued that when "revelation, and philosophy, and public experience, and all other grounds of probability and demonstration have supplied us with matter, then reason does but make use of them: that is, in plain terms, there being so many ways of arguing, so many sects, such differing interests, and such variety of authority, so many pretenses, and so many false beliefs, it concerns every wise man to consider which is the best argument, which proposition relies upon the truest grounds."

If we would not be led through life as dumb cattle, controlled by falsehood and evil, then we must exercise the power of reason, that power with which God has endowed us and which makes us human. Our liberty as a nation and as individuals depends to a large extent upon our ability to reason and thus to make reasonable judgments, judgments others can understand. So Jeremy Taylor and William White believed.

To act as reasonable beings is not simple nor without dangers and problems. Cambridge Platonists in the seventeenth century veered toward the divinization of reason. One of their number claimed that "to go against reason is to go against God: It is the self-same thing, and to do that which the reason of the case doth require and that which God himself doth appoint. Reason is the Divine governor of man's life. It is the very voice of God." Such a statement assumes that reason is more than an instrument to deal with matters presented to the senses: It is itself a source of revelation.

To a certain extent Hooker would have agreed for the moral law of reason is from God. To violate its dictates is to go against God. But Hooker—and Anglicanism in general—emphasizes the corrupt nature of reason without grace. To go against natural reason that leads us astray is not, then, to go against God. Push the divinity of reason too far, and the necessity of special revelation—that to which Scripture and tradition testify—is obliterated. In the end God and the world are utterly divided, human reason reduced to amoral, quasi-mathematical deduction and to that quantitative inductive reasoning of physical science.

Rationalism in which reason is god, denying God's revelation in Scripture and tradition, arouses strong reactions from various sources, from pietists and romantics in diverse groups.

Militant rationalism provokes an equally militant irrationalism, and the two do battle to the detriment of the human enterprise. Rationalism is rightly opposed by Anglicans of whatever party or disposition who believe that insofar as human salvation and happiness are concerned, the only acceptable role for reason is in relation to Scripture and tradition, a relation that in common experience is dynamic, involving tension and the give and take of persons of diverse persuasions living not in perpetual animosity but in continuous, creative dialogue.

In that dialogue, those who defend the proper and necessary function of reason are sometimes labeled "liberal." Kenneth Cauthen has defined religious liberalism in America in terms of (1) belief in continuity, not disjunction, between God and the world, God acting in the world and in human personality; (2) the autonomy of human reason and experience involving rejection of arbitrary appeal to external authority; and (3) dynamism, involving a view of the world as changing and growing. The Anglican liberal—if he or she is to remain Anglican—respects the work of reason not as autonomous, but as related to Scripture and tradition.

The Anglican demands reasons from those who would saddle the Christian community with arbitrary dictates of authority, whether spiritual, institutional, or personal. We will not allow ourselves to be irrationally imposed upon. We ask questions, searching questions of Scripture and tradition. We do so with respect for the power of the living Christ operative through them. We know the operation of that living power presupposes the operation of our reason and therefore we dare to ask questions.

In the Episcopal Church liberalism has been associated since the latter half of the nineteenth century with the so-called Broad Church school, more a point of view than a school or party. Some people have considered Phillips Brooks (1835-93) to be its most prestigious member although he probably never departed very far from his early Evangelical convictions. He once denied he was a "Broad Churchman," but with others who bore that label he rejected the Evangelical theory of the inspiration of Scripture, the separation of sacred and secular, the failure to recognize truth in non-Christians and indifference to intellectual culture. As A. V. G. Allen said, Brooks and others of Broad Church persuasion "held with Hooker and Bishop [Joseph] Butler [of Durham] that the human reason was the God-given faculty for verifying the divine revelation."

Belief in the importance of reason could and did lead to further considerations, not the least of which concerns the importance of education for Anglicans. If reason is to be capable of good judgment; if reason is to be a faithful interpreter of Scripture and tradition; if reason is to judge the spirits wisely; if it is to put all authority to the test of rationality: it must be nurtured and developed. Episcopalians are a people who value learning.

Among the first tasks the Church faced after its organization in 1789 was provision of adequate education. Sunday schools started in 1814. Adult education began at about the same time with the publication of edifying magazines. The Convention of 1804 brought theological education under control, and in 1817 the General Theological Seminary was founded in New York City, the first Episcopal school for the education of clergy.

Anglicans have always been concerned about general education, and in this country colleges and secondary schools were founded under ecclesiastical auspices and became influential beyond their size and number in the nation's leadership. Such commitment to education, extending to encouragement of learning in the Church as a whole, reflects the importance the Church has ascribed to cultivation of the mind and training of godly reason in all people, both in the Church and in society at large.

While condemning intellectual arrogance, this Church rightly seeks to raise up a people who use their reason to the greatest extent possible, limited only by physical, psychological, and social barriers beyond its control. This Church encourages its people to understand the Scriptures, benefiting from the best fruits of historical/biblical criticism. It insists that all its members learn to distinguish between things essential to salvation and things indifferent. It urges its people to pursue learning in the sciences and the humanities as a part of Christian vocation, learning what they can of their history and culture and the physical world so their reason may be as informed as possible in making judgments.

This Church emphasizes reason, however, as guided by the Holy Spirit in order that all may know the limits of reason as well as its powers and appreciate Pascal's dictum: "The heart has its reasons, which reason does not know." Redeemed reason makes way for the recognition and expression of that yearning after God to which Scripture and tradition witness.

Episcopalians are a people required to make decisions governing their lives. The Church seeks to furnish the individual conscience—which is the mind governed by a rule—with all the resources needed to make responsible choices in the exercise of Christian liberty. This admittedly places a burden on our people, but we consider such a burden preferable to an authoritarianism which dictates what people should or should not do in every particular situation.

The Church's liturgy, with the preaching of God's Word and the administration of God's visible words, the sacraments; education both religious and general; the corporate life of the parish—all inform the Christian's mind, enabling it to exercise right reason and do what in conscience must be done. We need not stress here that this is not individualistic for all along we have noted that the struggle to maintain the right relationship between Scripture, tradition, reason and experience, between authority and liberty, is one that occurs among people as well as within them. In many ways the liturgy speaks to the importance of reason.

Bishop White pointed to the collect for Whitsunday which he said "supposes an operation of the human intellect distinct from immediate revelation." In the 1979 *Book of Common Prayer* that collect begins, "O God, who on this day taught the hearts of your faithful people by sending to them the light of your Holy Spirit: Grant us by the same Spirit to have a right judgment in all things . . ."

Chapter 5. Active Charity Bolsters Faith

We test our faith
in the world.

In our day to find experience mentioned alongside Scripture, tradition and reason in discussions of Anglican authority is not surprising. We live, after all, in an age of science. Empiricism, according to Paul van Buren in *The Secular Meaning of the Gospel,* is the essence of the modern spirit and requires that any viable faith be verifiable in an empirical sense.

The fact that we do not find experience specifically noted by Cranmer, Hooker and other sixteenth century Anglican divines does not mean it did not exist. The rise of Anglicanism in sixteenth and seventeenth century England coincided with the rise of modern science. John Ray, an Anglican clergyman until the Restoration in the seventeenth century and a world-renowned naturalist, affirmed *The Wisdom of God Manifested in the Works of Creation.* He found that empirical observation over years of experience on earth confirmed the basic truth of the Church's teachings about God. In Ray's writings we observe the beginnings of natural theology as influenced by empiricism. We also observe that this theology is rooted in a profound respect for the world and its contents, including humans, a respect permeating the theology of Hooker and those who followed him. Experience as an element of authority for what we believe and do extends further.

No one definition will please everyone, but William Temple (1881-1944), the Archbishop of Canterbury who so influenced Anglicans in America and everywhere, possessed an understanding that expresses most nearly what we are considering here. Religious experience, Temple teaches, is the entire experience of religious persons. It is life as lived in relation to God and involves not only prayer, but our work, recreation, eating, drinking and all else. Experience is thus life as lived in relation to a particular religious tradition, encountered in a particular community of religious persons. We are accustomed to hearing of a religious experience or experiences. Temple does not deny the existence of moments of special intensity, "but those moments derive their chief importance from the fact that they bring specially vivid awareness of what is matter of constant apprehension."

T. S. Eliot, the modern poet and critic, expressed much the same insight in *The Four Quartets.* He began with a particular religious experience—a divine annunciation in the rose garden of Burnt Norton where "the pool was filled with water out of sunlight." It was a moment of intense awareness. The emphasis seems to dwell on the unique, the singular, the "mountain-top" experience. The *Quartets* end with the realization that ordinarily our experience of the divine is encompassed in holy routine—"prayer, observation, discipline, thought, and action." That routine experience ultimately has just as much meaning and is far more dependable than the intense experience which could not be without the reality of the holy routine.

We should not lose sight of the fact that however we describe experience, whether in terms of the unique or the routine, it is as a writer in *Foundations,* an important group study of Christianity and modern thought published in 1914, said: "Faith persists only in so far as it finds adequate—though never complete—justification in experience." Not that faith must be verified in all its aspects or that we must find justification for all its teachings in experience immediately known to each of us, but we must have some experience to bolster our faith or else we submit to arbitrary authority or are hypocrites.

Anglicanism has a strong basis for making these assertions. *The Book of Common Prayer* and the teachings of Richard Hooker in defense and explanation of the Prayer Book focus upon participation. To be a Christian—and thus also to be a member of a Church—is to participate in Christ. This means to live in faithful relationship to the Trinity—to goodness, wisdom and power. Word and sacraments, life together in the Spirit, inform our daily lives to the extent that we not only test the spirits through our experience, but also more and more deeply participate in Christ—through our experience.

To feed the hungry, clothe the naked, provide shelter for the homeless, visit the sick and those in prison is to minister to Christ. For as we learn from Matthew 25, Christ is present in those who confront us with their needs. So to minister is to participate in Christ's ministry, Christ through us reaching out to those in need. To live in such a way is to experience life in Christ and to be confirmed in one's faith. Anglicanism is practical and thus focuses attention on experience, on a life of active charity in the world.

Experience also involves such worldly wisdom as helps us to make sense of reality and to live together in peace with justice. This kind of experience in turn influences the way we interpret Scripture and tradition. William White, first Bishop of Pennsylvania, was imbued with the Enlightenment outlook of his day and thus emphasized reason as the instrument for understanding revelation. The new "science" of sociology inspired the formation of the Social Gospel in America and caused such Episcopalians as W. D. P. Bliss and Bernard Iddings Bell to find in the Gospel the basis for the development of socialism.

The civil rights movement of the 1950s and later provided a fresh, sometimes disturbing and sometimes exhilarating, understanding of Scripture and tradition. The long struggle for women's rights and ultimately for liberation inspired Vida Scudder to fight vigorously for a more realistic and humane interpretation of Scripture and tradition. The harsh realities of war in this century with the ultimate threat of nuclear holocaust, the diminishment of the world's resources along with accelerating population growth—all are experiences which influence our perception of the Christian faith. This is not surprising; nor is it something to be regretted. Indeed, if we believe with Temple that God is active in world process, or that God is involved in developing history, we dare not ignore the insights gained through human experience and must seek to understand that experience.

There are, of course, dangers in adopting some culturally influenced criteria for the interpretation of Scripture and tradition. It seems clear now, for instance, that Paul van Buren in *The Secular Meaning of the Gospel* went too far when, by applying the verification principle of modern science, he determined that language about God is meaningless. The principle itself has been challenged by secular linguists. The development psychology of Erik Erickson and others has been useful, but, when allowed to dominate our understanding of the Gospel, it perverts it. The current emphasis on pietistic or charismatic experience can distort the faith by limiting salvation to a select few with sufficient, discernible religious experience. The emphasis on self-identity and fulfillment in our society can bend the truth to serve the destructive narcissism of our time.

John Macquarrie, a convert to the Episcopal Church who once taught at Union Theological Seminary, New York, notes that "a proper balance must be maintained between the two formative factors of experience and revelation." We cannot believe in God revealed in and through Scripture and tradition without "some present firsthand experience of the holy while, on the other hand, the present experience" is "controlled and given its form by that revelation" and cannot be what it intends without revelation.

We might add here that the wisdom of the age in which we live, the scientific method, depth psychology, educational philosophy, space technology, and all the rest are to be taken seriously as we seek to understand God's acting in the world and history—but only as we are controlled and formed by revelation, by Scripture and tradition which constitute the firm core of Christian faith. To find and maintain this balance is never easy. Favoring one or the other is simpler. Our society does not help us to regard tension as good or creative, yet from the beginning of time tension has been so recognized.

One way to view the balance (or tension) is to recognize that despite our diversity we worship the one, true God. We are complex persons, products and makers of culture, members of different races, nationalities, creeds, with limited human capacities, conditioned by vastly differing environments, replete with diverse likes and dislikes, friends and enemies, failures and aspirations. Different as we are, we all encounter the one God of Scripture and tradition through our engagement in that holy routine that is ours in Prayer Book worship. We yearn for oneness with God—for truth, goodness and beauty. We yearn to participate in the divine goodness, wisdom and power but acknowledge that in this life such oneness, such participation, while actual, is never complete.

The poetry of George Herbert, John Donne, T.S. Eliot, and others is expressive of the tension in the midst of which we know such glory as passes human understanding and yet is explicable for in the Incarnation God "Hath deigned to chuse thee by adoption,/ Coheire to His glory and Sabbath's endlesse rest." That is to say that in the struggle with God, which is our experience of the holy, we find we are sustained by faith which is bred in the common life of the Church, the Church which is the Incarnate in and for the world. The Christian life is experience in the community of the Church and in the world the Church serves, experience which is controlled and formed by the revelation of the God who is truth, goodness and beauty.

I have said nothing thus far about the relation of experience to reason. Admittedly the distinction between the two is difficult to make, especially if we interpret reason broadly as the "moral law of reason" as in Hooker's *Lawes* or as redeemed by grace and guided by the Holy Spirit as in Bishop White's theology. Viewed thusly, reason is not just intellect or sound learning. It is the core of the knowing self without which we could not knowingly experience anything. Furthermore, such reason is active, on the basis of experience criticizing and reforming the present Church and world.

Having said this, we must admit we have been making a distinction of sorts. We experience and are thereby influenced or acted upon. Through reason we participate in experience, making judgments about it and influencing it. Experience needs the operation of reason if we are to be protected from error and evil. Hooker criticized those Puritans who on the basis of their experience claimed a direct pipeline to the Holy Spirit, requiring them to bring forth the reasons for their belief concerning their experience. Bishop White criticized Calvinists for claiming personal assurance of pardon from sin by the Holy Spirit directly, and he criticized Quakers who felt the impulse of the inner voice partly because he believed them to be misled by their emotions and partly because they seemed ignorant of the process of knowing.

Experience must meet the test of reason as well as being controlled and formed by Scripture and tradition. But then, too, we must insist that reason is not fully what it is meant to be until it finds outlet in experience, engaging the whole human being, emotions as well as intellect. Furthermore, the emphasis on experience helps to guard against the arrogance of reason for although experience must yield its reasons, it often surpasses the reach of intellect and passes into what we name mystery. This does not necessarily mean such experience is irrational; it is rational up to the point it exceeds the capabilities of human reason.

Temple believed individual religious experience—the experience of awe in the presence of the holy—is incommunicable. Such experience as T. S. Eliot's in the rose garden at Burnt Norton seemed to be so; yet for that experience to find fruition in action, it needed to be understood. The poet wrote of it in poetic language, bridging the mind and mystery in order to understand and that we might share that understanding to our benefit. Such understanding is not surprisingly difficult.

When immersed in the healthful interaction of Scripture, tradition, reason and experience, we must certainly recognize that although we may be grasped by God and influenced in the way of truth, goodness and beauty, we are yet finite beings whose perceptions are limited. Our proper attitude is that of humility in the presence of the divine—not such humility as results in resignation of our God-given reason and experience, our ability to criticize and create, but such humility as is expressed in awe, awe which anticipates such truth, goodness and beauty as surpass our reason and experience.

Richard Hooker expressed such awe when he wrote: "Whatsoever either men on earth, or the Angels of heaven do know, it is a drop of that unemptiable fountain of wisdom, which wisdom hath diversely imparted her treasures unto the world. As her ways are of sundry kinds, so her manner of teaching is not merely one and the same. Some things she openeth by the sacred books of Scripture; some things by the glorious works of nature; with some things she inspireth them from above by spiritual influence; in some things she leadeth and traineth them only by worldly experience and practice. We may not so in any special kind admire her that we disgrace her in any other, but let all her ways be according unto their place and degree adored."

Chapter 6. Knowing and Doing the Truth

By Scripture, Tradition, Reason
and Experience we seek to be Christians.

Episcopalians are people who seek to know and do the truth by means of the creative interplay of Scripture, tradition, reason and experience. That this is not easy must now be evident. Difficult though it may be, we acknowledge that without emphasis upon Scripture, tradition, reason and experience we are diminished as Episcopalians, as Christians, and as human beings.

We recognize that a certain priority exists among the four strands or elements. Scripture as the Word of God and Tradition as the conveyor of that Word are the vehicles of God's special revelation to restore us to a saving relationship with him. As such, Scripture and the Tradition aligned to it possess priority over reason and experience. Episcopalians revere the Scriptures for their revelation of God in Christ by the power of the Spirit. They revere all else—ministry, liturgy and teaching—to the degree it faithfully and powerfully conveys that Word of God to the present.

We must, however, acknowledge another priority, the priority of perception. We are first of all reasoning, experiencing people. God has created us as such. In and through our lives as humans—flawed and corrupt though we are—God is making known the law of the universe, the law of sacrificial love. As reasoning, experiencing humans we receive the revelation of God in Scripture and through tradition. Episcopalians honor the created order. We are humanists in the best sense. We care for the rights and responsibilities attached to our humanity, and we acknowledge our responsibility under God for the care and nurture of all creation. We are environmentalists in the best sense.

Human development, too, holds a priority. Richard Hooker wrote that by experience we know that what first teaches us to acknowledge the Scripture as God's Word "is the authority of God's Church. For when we know the whole Church of God hath that opinion of the Scripture, we judge it even at the first an impudent thing" to be of contrary opinion. "Afterward the more we bestow our labor in reading or hearing the mysteries thereof, the more we find that the thing itself doth answer our received opinion concerning it." Thus the Tradition, understood in terms of the Church's authority, comes first, conveying the Scripture to us, convincing us of its nature until by experience we affirm its truth for "the very thing hath ministered farther reason."

We are, then, as Episcopalians, people who revere Tradition and respect traditions. We love the Church for the Church teaches us how to love Christ, but we do not rest content on the Church's authority alone. In time, reason and experience must confirm what authority has provided.

The liturgy is one means by which the Church most powerfully conveys God's saving Word and nurtures us toward confirmation of what that Word conveys by its God-given authority. Our liturgy is a traditional means by which Scripture and Christ, as the culmination of scriptural witness, are conveyed to Christians from birth to death in every moment of their growth through life. *The Book of Common Prayer* is that historical form of liturgy which not only presents Christ to us, but by God's grace enables us to perceive Christ through what constitutes our humanity: reason and experience. No wonder, then, Episcopalians revere the Prayer Book. Generation after generation of folk, common and great, have been nurtured by the holy routine of our common worship and have been made more truly human through participation in Christ, the beginning and the end of all that is true and beautiful and good in creation. That we become disturbed over liturgical revision is not surprising. The Prayer Book is intimately related to our lives.

The Church's ordained ministry assists us through preaching and interpreting Scripture, through leadership in liturgical worship, and through cultivation of an atmosphere and ethos in which reasoning, experiencing people encounter Christ and one another in significant—if at times tense and frustrating—dialogue. The parish priest is much like the orchestra conductor whose task is to interpret the composer's score in such a way that the musicians will produce music that will affect and change each orchestra member as well as the audience. To do that, the conductor must know each instrument, each performer, and be sensitive to what will bring forth results that surpass anyone's expectation. Episcopalians revere the ordained ministry for its faithful communication of Christ and its sensitive care that the people so receive Christ that they in turn witness to him in ministry to one another, to the clergy, and to those who do not know him.

We have observed that the relation of the four poles—Scripture, tradition, reason and experience—is dynamic, both within ourselves and in the Church. We have noted that the parties of the Church—Evangelical, Catholic, Liberal—emphasize some one element but always in relation to the others. We must stress here the value of the creative tension which exists not only between the parties of the Church, but also within ourselves and within the parish church—even within the parties. To preserve and extend the richness of our tradition we need not hide differences and keep peace so much as accept creative tension, assure constant dialogue, and anticipate gain from whatever conflict occurs within the orbit of mutual respect and love.

Christianity affirms the unity of opposites in Christ. T. S. Eliot spoke to this when he wrote:

The dance along the artery
The circulation of the lymph
Are figured in the drift of stars
Ascend to summer in the tree
We move above the moving tree
In light upon the figured leaf
And hear upon the sodden floor
Below, the boarhound and the boar
Pursue their pattern as before
But reconciled among the stars.

In spite of all appearances to the contrary, all that exists fits into a pattern, an order, a wholeness from which all that is comes and in which all that is is made complete. Knowing this, Episcopalians are not distraught by differences unless such differences result in breaking the essential bond of love and end in schism. We acknowledge the richness of our tradition and take seriously what those who differ from us say and do.

This, of course, challenges the Episcopal Church and all its members. We are too often less than our tradition calls us to be. We need, therefore, to enter more deeply into the holy routine, the ceaseless rhythm of contrition and thanksgiving in which we shall be nurtured, our hearts purified, our sight cleared, our minds strengthened.

Worship is essential if we are to be what we claim to be, but education is important, too. What are we doing in our church schools? What are we doing when we engage in adult education? Do we see Christian education as a compartment separate from the whole, or do we see it connected to the very heart of our Christian lives? To live creatively as guided by Scripture, tradition, reason and experience we must be educated, led into ever more serious and comprehensive understanding of the faith once given to the saints and still the most vital power in the world. Through education we learn to use our reason, as we have seen, in the reception and transmission of the Christ and we learn to test our experience against that Revelation, to discern the spirits and to avoid the spirits of this age which would destroy us. Committed as we are to Scripture, tradition, reason and experience, the Episcopal Church's basic education in this age should be structured and conducted in terms of the creative interplay of the four vital elements.

Educated to be faithful, reasoning Christians, nurtured by worship in community, we shall be equipped to encounter the issues that confront this age. Not that we shall then possess all the answers, but we shall have assurance of the direction in which to go toward the resolution of our problems, global and personal. The looming, ominous threat of global nuclear war, the problems involved in distributing our earthly resources equitably both in relation to people and to the ecosystem, the constant threat to the consciousness-center personality in an age of technology—high and low—may frighten us, but they do not so overwhelm us that we are paralyzed.

We know the most consequential thing we can do is to witness to Christ, who reveals the law of our gens and kind to be gentleness and kindness—sacrifical love. Through the exercise of reason, on the basis of experience, we witness to Christ in the midst of all that threatens us, knowing that the resolution of our problems is in that resolution of all existence where the people of God meet at the heavenly banquet in the presence of Christ the Lord.

This does not prevent us from dealing realistically and productively with what confronts us. Grounded in Christ, we make use of all the worldly wisdom available, acknowledge the necessity of making decisions which are full of ambiguities and which are harmful as well as helpful. Such realism is supported not only by the ultimate vision Christians possess, but also by the holy routine in which we confess our sins and are forgiven, renewed to keep on working for the realization of Christ's commonwealth on earth.

This is what it means to be an Episcopalian: to be guided by Scripture, tradition, reason and experience in proper proportion and creative tension. As we grow in relation to the operation of Scripture, tradition, reason and experience, we participate in what transcends our particular tradition, we become ever more ecumenical and stand ready to enrich the great, diverse, complex commonwealth of Churches unified in Christ their source and their end.

To be an Episcopalian is not to stand aside arrogantly proclaiming our superiority to others, but to recognize our riches and our needs and to so grow in our tradition that we surmount the particular tradition of Anglicanism through participation in *the* Tradition which is Christ the Savior of all. By commitment to a common life governed by respect for Scripture, tradition, reason and experience, Episcopalians declare their commitment to the realization of oneness in Christ together with other Christians.

In the end, all Christians, of whatever denomination, seek to live as guided by Scripture, tradition, reason and experience. Each denomination has its own way of doing so; thus, in a sense, ecumenicity consists in the dialogue of traditions among the Churches, traditions all acknowledging the importance of Scripture, tradition, reason and experience.

Christians of whatever denomination are people who hallow, bless and sanctify the Lord—Christ—in their hearts (I Pet. 3:15), by the grace of God "growing up in every way into him who is the head, into Christ, from whom the whole body, joined and knit together by every joint with which it is supplied" (Eph.4:15-16), guided through the instruments of Scripture, tradition, reason and experience, creatively, dynamically alive, and interacting in each person and in the Church.